PACs, Super PACs, and Fundraising

David Petechuk

Eldorado Ink
PO Box 100097
Pittsburgh, PA 15233
www.eldoradoink.com

Produced by OTTN Publishing, Stockton, New Jersey

CPSIA compliance information: Batch#MAP2016.
For further information, contact Eldorado Ink at info@eldoradoink.com.

First printing

1 3 5 7 9 8 6 4 2

Library of Congress Cataloging-in-Publication Data

Names: Petechuk, David, author.
Title: PACs, super PACs, and fundraising / David Petechuk.
Description: Pittsburgh, PA : Eldorado Ink, 2016. | Series: American politics
 today | Includes bibliographical references and index. | Description based
 on print version record and CIP data provided by publisher; resource not
 viewed.
Identifiers: LCCN 2015048943 (print) | LCCN 2015048680 (ebook) | ISBN
 9781619001176 (ebook) | ISBN 9781619000933 (hc) | ISBN 9781619001015 (pb)
 | ISBN 9781619001091 (trade)
Subjects: LCSH: Political action committees—United States—Juvenile
 literature. | Campaign funds—United States—Juvenile literature. | United
 States—Politics and government—1989-   —Juvenile literature.
Classification: LCC JK1991 (print) | LCC JK1991 .P47 2016 (ebook) | DDC
 324/.40973—dc23
LC record available at http://lccn.loc.gov/2015048943

*For information about custom editions, special sales, or premiums,
please contact our special sales department at info@eldoradoink.com.*

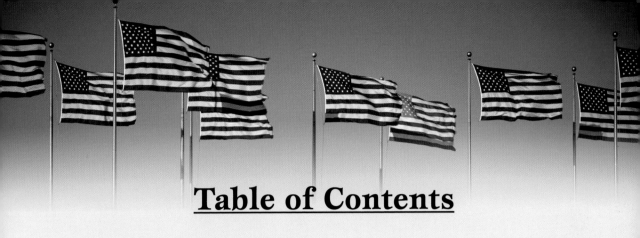

Table of Contents

Chapter 1

Money and Politics

T he debate over the influence of money in politics has a long history in the United States. Although it seems to have reached a crescendo in the twenty-first century, concerns over this issue in American politics date back to George Washington's day. The concern then, however, was not about large sums of money being donated to a candidate's campaign. Rather, alarm bells went off when candidates were thought to be buying votes.

Not only is George Washington the father of the United States, he is also the father of campaign finance reform. In 1775 Washington lost an election to the Virginia House of Burgesses. Two years later, and one year after the United States won its independence, he had an idea. Washington held a buffet at the polling booth that included a barrel of punch, thirty-five gallons of wine, forty-three gallons of strong cider, and dinner for his friends. The cost was about $195 into today's dollars.

A man holds a sign denouncing the influence of money in the American political system during a protest in New York City. Many experts believe that the 2016 presidential campaign will set records for campaign fundraising and spending, with a total possibly exceeding $5 billion.

In 2015, defense contractors like Lockheed Martin, Honeywell International, and Northrop Grumman were among the largest contributors to political campaigns.

Washington won the election, beating his opponent, Captain Thomas Swearingen, by a count of 310 to 45. However, Washington's new colleagues in the Virginia House of Burgesses were not impressed. As noted in a 2014 *Washington Post* article by James Fuller, the Virginia House of Burgesses quickly passed a law barring candidates "or any persons on their behalf" from supplying potential voters with "money, meat, drink, entertainment or provision or . . . any present, gift, reward or entertainment etc. in order to be elected."

EARLY POLITICAL CAMPAIGNS

Following the American Revolution, which ended in 1783, candidates for the U.S. presidency initially did not even conduct political campaigns. Campaigning was considered beneath the dignity of the office. This view changed as political parties grew stronger and the Industrial Revolution brought about transportation, improved communications,

Election ticket for Andrew Jackson and his running mate John C. Calhoun from the 1828 presidential election. The names listed below are Democratic Party candidates from various Ohio counties. The straw broom pictured at the top was a traditional symbol of reform, indicating that the candidates would "clean up" government corruption.

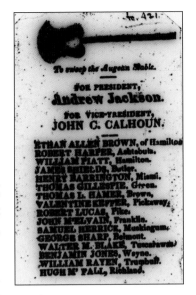

and new jobs. Candidates for political offices could no longer rely on personally interacting with voters. They now had to garner support by means of rallies, caucuses, and conventions.

Even before the Industrial Revolution, however, big money was being spent on campaigns for state-level offices. A congressional campaign in the Midwest or mid-Atlantic regions in the early 1800s could cost as much as $4,000, which was a significant amount of money at the time. Campaigns for state-level offices also typically required five-figure sums. The money was spent on newspaper ads, pamphlets, and various campaign items and events, such as floats, coonskin caps, and revival meetings, all designed to sway voters to support particular candidates.

Andrew Jackson was one of the first U.S. politicians to run a political campaign that could be compared to a modern campaign. In his run to become president in 1828, Jackson organized a campaign staff charged with raising money and getting out the vote. The organization was so sophisticated that it included committees to coordinate rallies and parades. On Election Day, twice as many voters turned out, compared to previous elections. Ironically, in his farewell address as president in 1837, he warned of the insidiousness of "money power" in politics.

Just thirty years later, in 1858, Abraham Lincoln's campaign for the U.S. Senate made it clear that running for office was going to require a significant flow of cash from donors. Except for $500 from wealthy donors, Lincoln financed his Senate campaign out of his own pocket. As a result, Lincoln ended up declaring bankruptcy. His law practice saved him from permanent poverty. Lincoln subsequently earned enough money to buy an Illinois newspaper to support his run for the 1860 presidential election. Business leaders from Philadelphia and New York City also funded his successful presidential campaign.

THE GROWTH OF CAMPAIGN FUNDRAISING

Over the years, the costs of conducting a political campaign, especially at the statewide and national level, have skyrocketed. That does not mean that early campaigns were inexpensive or unsophisticated.

By the mid-1800s, national political committees could spend up to $100,000 on a presidential campaign. In the meantime, the size and cost of government were growing, attracting more businesspeople to become campaign donors in hopes of furthering their interests. Following the Civil War, political parties were gathering large donations from the wealthy, such as the Vanderbilts and the Astors. Furthermore, federal government employees were required to donate part of their salary to national campaigns.

The Naval Appropriations Bill, passed in 1867, forbade politicians and their political parties from requiring navy yard workers to make political donations. In 1883 the Civil Service Reform Act, also known as the Pendleton Bill, was passed, applying the Naval Appropriations Bill to all government workers. Although these bills protected workers from being forced to contribute to political campaigns, it ultimately led the political parties to seek other sources of funding, primarily donations from wealthy individuals and corporations.

The 1896 presidential election reached a new high in campaign financing. William McKinley, the Republican candidate, spent $7 million on his successful campaign, compared to the $650,000 spent by his Democratic opponent, William Jennings Bryan. The chairman of the Republican National Committee at the time was Marcus Alonzo Hanna. Working to get McKinley elected, Hanna put in place the groundwork for modern political campaigns. He sought campaign contributions from businesses and introduced the concept of political advertising, including printing 300,000 flyers, in nine different languages, urging people to vote for McKinley.

LEGISLATING CAMPAIGN FINANCING

Following McKinley's assassination in 1901, his vice-president, Theodore Roosevelt, took office. Roosevelt quickly became known as a trustbuster who was opposed to corporate influence in politics. Ironically, however, Roosevelt turned to bankers and industrialists to help support his 1904 reelection campaign for president.

Even though Roosevelt won the 1904 election in a landslide, public opinion about the incumbent president changed. The public believed that he was liable to be unduly influenced by his large campaign donors. During his 1905 address to the U.S. Congress, Roosevelt said he supported a law that would prohibit corporations from making contributions to any political committee, no matter what the committee's purpose.

William McKinley's 1896 presidential campaign was run by Ohio businessman Mark Hanna, who raised money, opened campaign offices in every state, and produced literature like the poster above that encouraged voters to elect the Republican to the White House.

Roosevelt also proposed a system of public financing for all federal candidates' campaigns. Two years later, in 1907, Roosevelt renewed his call for public financing of political campaigns, and the U.S. Congress passed the Tillman Act, banning bank and corporate giving. The act, however, went largely unenforced. Several other acts would be passed over the next five decades seeking to regulate campaign financing. These acts called for limiting spending by U.S. House of Representatives and Senate candidates, limiting contributions to campaigns by federal workers and contractors, and prohibiting labor unions from directly contributing to federal candidates. The Taft-Hartley Act of 1947 banned unions, corporations, and interstate banks from contributing to federal candidates' campaigns.

Despite various laws to control who finances federal campaigns and to reduce outside influences in politics, circumstances often increased candidates' need to seek more outside contributions. For example, women gained the right to vote with the passage of the

The Power of the Media

When John Kennedy and Richard Nixon appeared in the first televised presidential debate during the 1960 presidential campaign, Kennedy looked calm, cool, and collected, like a leader who could deal with a crisis. On the other hand, Richard Nixon looked pale and could be seen sweating profusely under the bright camera lights. Kennedy won the election, and politicians took notice. A new era in political campaigning had begun.

It was no longer just about the message. If a candidate could come across well in the media, especially on television, the candidate could sway a wide swath of the electorate. The costs of media consultants and television advertising contribute to a growing emphasis on garnering campaign dollars.

In June 2012, President Barack Obama spent 63 percent of his $57 million campaign budget for the month on media. His opponent, Mitt Romney, spent 39 percent of his $27 million budget for the month on media advertising and related expenses. The disparity and Obama's victory only reinforced the power of media in politics.

The media not only helps candidates get elected but can also influence the amount of financial support a potential candidate receives. If a candidate is treated negatively in the media or largely ignored, it can greatly affect that candidate's ability to raise campaign funds. Potential contributors may look elsewhere for more viable candidates.

Democrat Hillary Clinton speaks at a union event in Nevada during her 2016 presidential campaign. The Federal Election Campaign Act prohibits corporations and labor unions from contributing from their general treasury funds to candidates in federal elections. Spending on campaigns must be done from a separate fund that is segregated from the general treasury and designated for political action. In the United States, union PACs tend to support Democratic Party candidates.

Nineteenth Amendment to the Constitution in 1920. That gave political candidates both a new and a significantly broader constituency to address and they needed more money to do so.

SKYROCKETING CAMPAIGN COSTS

As the U.S. population and the number of voters grew, so did the need for more campaign financing. From 1956 to 1968, the cost of running a national campaign doubled, from $155 million to more than $300 million. Much of the increase was due to the growth of broadcast media, especially since television had shown its impact on elections during 1960 presidential debates. Spending on advertising and other media-related costs had grown from $10 million to $60 million in just over a decade.

In 1971, the U.S. Congress passed the Federal Election Campaign Act (FECA), which set limits on individual contributions and increased public disclosure of campaign receipts. FECA was amended in 1974, following the Watergate scandal and the resignation of President Richard Nixon. The amendment to FECA greatly limited how much individuals could contribute to federal candidates and also placed further spending limits on federal elections.

Between 1978 and 1990, spending on federal election campaigns rose from $153.5 million to $402.7 million. From this point on, political operatives focused more and more of their energies on fundraising. Eventually, political action committees, more commonly known by the acronym PACs, became increasingly important because donors could contribute more money to PACs than to individual campaigns and political parties. PACs led to the growing concern that rich donors, including corporations, now had more power than individual small donors to influence elections.

In 2010, the U.S. Supreme Court overturned most of the campaign finance laws in the United States through the *Citizens United v. the Federal Election Commission* ruling. The result was the birth of the super PAC. The new influx of money led to $6.2 billion being spent on races for president and for the U.S. Congress in 2012.

In 2014 the Supreme Court struck down the caps on how much individuals can donate to federal campaigns and political parties over a two-year period. An estimated $4 billion was spent on campaigns for the 2014 midterm elections, and it was estimated that all the candidates running for president in 2016 spent more than $5 billion combined. With campaign financing reaching into the millions and billions of dollars, contentious debates have erupted about the role of money in politics.

Beyond the obvious issue of influencing candidates' decisions once they are elected, the need to raise huge sums of money requires office-holders to spend time and energy at fundraising events. As candidates devote more and more time to raising campaign cash, some observers believe the high cost of running a campaign detracts from officials' ability to do the job they were elected to do—namely, to govern.

Chapter 2

Money Matters: The Basics

In an ideal world, politicians would base their campaigns on ideas and policies. In today's world of politics, money may matter just as much.

For the most part, research has shown that whoever spends the most money on a campaign in a federal election wins that election. For example, in the 2014 elections, 94 percent of the largest spenders in races for the House of Representatives won. In the Senate races, 82 percent of the biggest spenders won, up from 76 percent in the 2012 elections.

Although winning candidates spend more on their elections than those who lose, money is not everything. For example, a candidate's charisma and his or her position on policies still count for a lot. As noted by Bob Shrum, a senior fellow at New York University's Robert F. Wagner Graduate School of Public Service, on the Freakonomics website: "Big money without the right message can become a penny waiting for change."

Nevertheless, it costs a lot to run for office in the United States, especially for national office. In 2012 the combined amount of money spent by both the Democratic and Republican presidential candidates broke the $2 billion mark. In the year before the 2016 election for president, the estimated cost of running the Democratic and Republican campaigns was expected to be close to $5 billion. To run for president, the Senate, or the House of Representatives, estimated start-up costs alone for a campaign are around $10 million. The majority of the money goes for overhead and efforts focusing on raising more money.

Running for statewide and local offices, such as state governor or the mayor of a major city, is also expensive. In 2010, Rick Perry spent more than $41 million to win the Texas governorship, and Jerry Brown's campaign spent $36.6 in his successful 2010 campaign to become governor of California. The least money spent by a winning gubernatorial campaign in 2010 was $513,698, spent by Sean Parnell in Alaska. Even running for the mayor of a large or moderately sized city is expensive. In 2012, two candidates running for mayor of San Diego, California, spent more than $10 million combined. Running for mayor of a medium-size city typically costs close to $1 million or more.

So how are national campaigns run and where do they get their financing?

PRIVATE FUNDING

There are four general categories of campaign contributors. The first two categories are small and large individual donors. Determining the difference between a small and a large donor is somewhat subjective, depending on who is making the donation and who is defining the contributions as large or small. According to the Federal Election Commission (FEC), small individual contributors are those who contribute $200 or less. Large individual donors contribute more than $200.

The third category of campaign contributors includes political action committees (PACS) and other groups that collect donations from outside donors. In the 2014 election cycle, special types of PACs, called super PACs, raised nearly $700 million and spent almost $350 million of it on the elections, although none of that money was directly contributed to a candidate's campaign. In the final category are

In 2015, when wealthy businessman Donald Trump entered the race for president, he initially declared that he would self-finance his campaign so that he would not need to raise money from lobbyists or special interest groups. This appealed to unhappy voters, who believed politicians from both parties were beholden to those who contributed to their campaigns.

wealthy candidates who finance much of their campaign with their own money. For example, in 2009 Michael Bloomberg spent $109 million of his own money to get reelected mayor of New York City.

For the most part, the least amount of money overall comes from small individual donors and rich candidates who finance their own elections. The vast majority of donations come from large individual donors and groups like PACs. In the 2012 federal election cycle, more than a quarter of the nearly $6 billion in contributions from identified sources came from just 31,385 individuals, which is equal to one ten-thousandth of the U.S. population.

Nevertheless, small donors can still make an impact. In Barack Obama's reelection campaign for president during the 2011–2012 election cycle, nearly half the individual donors to his campaign gave $200 or less.

SPENDING LIMITS

The FEC has set various spending limits on donating to a federal election and, in some cases, campaign expenditures are limited as well. These limits are part of campaign finance reform, an effort to control the influence of money in politics and political campaigns. Every two years, the FEC updates its contribution limits based on inflation.

The government and the courts have passed and ruled on various laws and acts relating to campaign financing. These laws change the rules for campaign financing and have been hotly debated over the years. For example, in the *Citizens United v. FEC* Supreme Court case in 2010, the High Court essentially struck down limits on the total amount of money organizations could contribute to political action committees. In a later case that year, the justices struck down limits on how much large individual donors could give to independent political organizations. To some, this meant that rich donors had gained too much influence in deciding campaign outcomes. In addition, the public believes elected officeholders may be obligated to support the agendas of their largest contributors, even if taking positions in support of those contributors' agendas runs contrary to the public good.

HARD MONEY VERSUS SOFT MONEY

Each of the major political parties in the United States has a national committee that oversees various aspects of a campaign, including fundraising. In addition to the Democratic National Committee and the Republican National Committee, these committees include the Reform Party National Committee, the Libertarian Party National Committee, and the Green Party National Committee. The national committees also work with state-level committees to help party candidates get elected to state and local offices.

Individuals and organizations, such as companies and unions, can donate money either to a political party or to a specific candidate. National committees typically divide these donations into two types—"hard money" and "soft money." Hard money refers to contributions that are regulated by campaign finance laws enforced by the FEC. These contributions are directed toward a specific candidate or a candidate's campaign. Hard money typically comes from individuals or a PAC.

Soft money refers to contributions that are unregulated and unlimited. However, soft money is not allowed to be used for a specific candidate's election campaign. Soft money can be donated for efforts such as voter registration, get-out-the-vote drives, and advocating the passage of a particular law. These funds come from individuals and PACs, just like hard money.

The Bipartisan Campaign Reform Act of 2002, also known as the McCain-Feingold Act, essentially banned soft money financing or donations for general party-building activities. Under the act's provisions, all donations to national candidates or parties were more strictly regulated and essentially had to come in

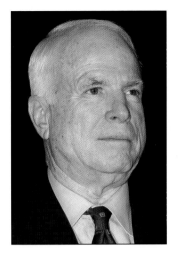

The 2002 Bipartisan Campaign Reform Act, sponsored by Senators John McCain (R-AZ; left) and Russ Feingold (D-WI) prohibited large campaign contributions by wealthy individuals and corporations to national party committees. It was thought that this legislation would reduce the influence of money in politics, as campaigns would have to rely on small donors. However, the ban on "soft money" left individual and corporate donors free to donate funds to outside groups, such as PACs, that tend to be more extreme in their views than the national party organizations.

the form of hard money. However, state party committees could still accept soft money if the donations complied with an individual state's law.

TWO GAME-CHANGING COURT CASES

In a U.S. constitutional law case, known popularly as *Citizens United*, the U.S. Supreme Court made a ruling that changed the fundamentals of campaign financing. The case involved a group called Citizens United. In 2008 the organization had produced a film critical of Hillary Clinton, who at the time was running for the Democratic Party's presidential nomination in the party primaries, and wanted to advertise the film on television. To do so, Citizens United would have had to violate the 2002 Bipartisan Campaign Reform Act. This act

The Power of the Internet

The Internet has become a significant factor in campaign strategy. Over the first decade of the twenty-first century, the Internet also appeared to be gaining popularity as a way of raising small contributions from numerous donors. For example, during his 2004 Republican primary campaign for president, Ron Paul raised $4 million online in one day. In his 2008 campaign for the U.S. presidency, Barack Obama collected $36 million in the month of January, primarily through small donations made online.

The benefits of seeking contributions online are twofold. It is a relatively inexpensive way to solicit contributions and can reach a significant number of people throughout the country or a particular state. In other words, candidates can use the Internet to raise funds quickly and cheaply.

With Supreme Court rulings like *Citizens United*, however, the continued practice of Internet fundraising, geared to soliciting small donations, may be in doubt. Campaigns and outside organizations, such as super PACs, are looking more and more toward mega donations from the super rich and are far less concerned about trying to get a lot of small donations via the Internet.

The Internet, however, is not going to go away as an approach for reaching numerous voters and garnering campaign contributions. For example, in his campaign to win the Democratic presidential nomination in 2016, U.S. Senator Bernie Sanders had raised nearly $9 million online by June 2015. That was more than any Republican primary candidate raised via the Internet.

Bernie Sanders skillfully used his website to collect donations from those who supported his campaign.

included a provision that outlawed expenditures by corporations and unions earmarked for "electioneering communication" that mentioned a candidate within sixty days of a general election or thirty days of a primary.

The High Court ruled that, according to the First Amendment provision of free speech, it was unconstitutional for the government to restrict nonprofit organizations from spending as much as they wanted in support of a candidate, including on television and by means of other advertisements mentioning a candidate. The only caveat was that these organizations could not coordinate their activities with a party or a candidate.

However, the federal ban on direct contributions from corporations or unions to a campaign or political party remained in place. Although still prohibited from contributing directly to candidates for national office, corporations, unions, and other organizations could contribute unlimited sums to other political organizations, such as super PACs and 501(c)(4)s, groups considered to be primarily social welfare organizations.

On April 2, 2014, the U.S. Supreme Court issued another ruling that significantly affected campaign financing. In *McCutcheon v. FEC*, the Supreme Court struck down the aggregate limits on the amount an individual could contribute to all federal candidates, parties, and PACs combined, over a two-year period. As in the *Citizens United* case, the High Court ruled that biennial aggregate limits were unconstitutional, according to the First Amendment and its freedom-of-speech clause.

As a result, the previous $123,200 aggregate limit on major donor contributions to federal candidates, party committees, and PACs, combined, was no longer applicable. Previously these limits were $48,600 combined to all federal candidates and $74,600 to all parties and PACs. Although limits still remained in place on how much individual donors could contribute to a single candidate's campaign ($2,700 per election), these donors were now able to contribute up to that amount to every single candidate for Congress, as well as even higher amounts to all so-called "leadership PACs," and to every national and state political party committee. Essentially, candidates were now able to band together to raise large sums from the same individuals through legal entities called "joint fundraising committees," which could then split up the money among various candidates.

McCutcheon v. FEC did not overturn all contribution limits enshrined in law over the years. For example, there were still limits on donations to individual candidates' campaigns. In addition, rules concerning full disclosure of campaign contributions and spending remained intact. Nevertheless, the *Citizens United* and *McCutcheon* decisions greatly weakened many campaign finance laws, especially those stemming from an amendment passed in 1974 to the Federal Election Campaign Act (FECA) of 1971 and from the Bipartisan Campaign Reform Act of 2002.

Many people contend that these two Supreme Court decisions gave the wealthy undue influence in the arena of political speech. In addition, some observers worry that the rulings will lead to the eventual deregulation of all campaign financing.

PUBLIC FUNDING

Public funding of campaigns refers to the ability of candidates to use money from federal and/or state treasuries to help fund their campaigns. The best-known form of public financing is the box taxpayers can check on their federal income tax return, sent to the Internal Revenue Service (IRS). By checking that box, taxpayers agree that $3 from their federal taxes should help support the campaigns of those running for president. Checking the box does not increase the taxpayer's tax bill or affect a tax refund.

Over the years, the number of people checking the campaign contribution box on the 1040 IRS form has dropped precipitously. In 1980 28.7 percent checked the campaign contribution box. In 2012 only 6.4 percent of those filing returns checked that box. Nevertheless, as of 2015, approximately $1.5 billion has gone to publicly financed candidates and nominating conventions since 1976, when the FEC instituted the first public funding of a presidential campaign.

In 2008 Barack Obama became the first person elected president since 1976 without accepting public funds. In 2012, no major candi-

Form **1040** Department of the Treasury—Internal Revenue Service (99)
U.S. Individual Income Tax Return 2014 OMB No. 1545-0074 | IRS Use Only—Do not write or staple in this space.

For the year Jan. 1–Dec. 31, 2014, or other tax year beginning , 2014, ending , 20 | See separate instructions.

Your first name and initial | Last name | Your social security number

If a joint return, spouse's first name and initial | Last name | Spouse's social security number

Home address (number and street). If you have a P.O. box, see instructions. | Apt. no. | ▲ Make sure the SSN(s) above and on line 6c are correct.

City, town or post office, state, and ZIP code. If you have a foreign address, also complete spaces below (see instructions).

Presidential Election Campaign
Check here if you, or your spouse if filing jointly, want $3 to go to this fund. Checking a box below will not change your tax or refund. ☐ You ☐ Spouse

Foreign country name | Foreign province/state/county | Foreign postal code

Filing Status
Check only one box.
1 ☐ Single
2 ☐ Married filing jointly (even if only one had income)
3 ☐ Married filing separately. Enter spouse's SSN above and full name here. ▶
4 ☐ Head of household (with qualifying person). (See instructions.) If the qualifying person is a child but not your dependent, enter this child's name here. ▶
5 ☐ Qualifying widow(er) with dependent child

Exemptions 6a ☐ **Yourself.** If someone can claim you as a dependent, **do not** check box 6a . . . . . | Boxes checked

The total amount of federal election funding in past election cycles has ranged from about $73 million in 1976 to nearly $240 million in 2000. In recent elections, the total has declined tremendously. In the 2012 election cycle, the federal government provided $37.9 million in public financing. That was a decline of more than $100 million from the 2008 election cycle's total of $139.5 million. The 2012 presidential election marked the first time that both the Republican and Democratic Party nominees opted out of the public financing program for both the primary and general elections.

date for the presidency accepted public funds. One of the principal reasons for rejecting such funding is the strict spending limits associated with this money. Presidential candidates believe those limits would put them at a disadvantage against an opponent who does not accept public financing and, therefore, raises more money for his or her campaign.

In April 2014, President Barack Obama signed legislation to end public funding of national nominating conventions for the presidency. The Obama administration argued that the funds could be better used elsewhere. Funds that had been set aside for nominating conventions were retargeted for medical research on childhood diseases, including cancer and autism.

STATE ELECTION FUNDING

As of 2015, twenty-five states had some form of public financing for election campaigns. In addition, major cities, such as New York and

Los Angeles, have adopted public financing programs. The public funding plans in states sometimes require a candidate who accepts public money to agree to a limit on how much the campaign spends on an election. They may also limit how much one group or individual contributes to a campaign.

The two main public funding programs in states are "clean election programs" and matching programs. As of 2015, only Arizona, Connecticut, and Maine had clean elections programs. These pro-

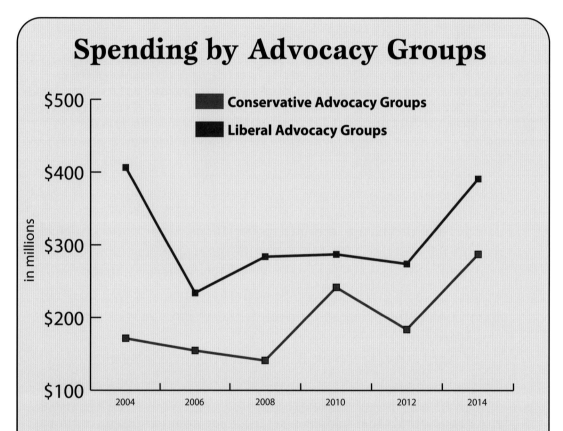

Spending by Advocacy Groups

Advocacy groups, formed under section 527 of the Internal Revenue Code, were originally formed to educate the public about particular political or social issues. They were not permitted to tell the public explicitly to elect or defeat a particular candidate until the Supreme Court's Citizens United *decision in 2010. Now, they may engage in the full range of political activity, including asking the public to vote for or against a would-be officeholder.*

Source: OpenSecrets.org.

In 2015, twenty-seven states allowed unlimited contributions to political parties. In addition, twelve states allowed unlimited contributions from individuals to state candidates.

grams typically require a candidate to demonstrate enough public support to warrant public funding for the campaign. Candidates show this support by collecting small contributions from a certain number of individuals, as mandated by the state. Once this level of support is demonstrated, the candidate can receive money equal to the expenditure limit set for the election in that state. New Mexico offers a similar program for judicial candidates only.

The second type of state public financing program provides matching funds for each qualifying contribution a candidate receives, up to a certain amount. The amount of public funding a candidate can receive is usually tied to expenditure limits set by the state legislators. In Hawaii, the program is funded through a tax return check-off, like the federal funding program.

How U.S. Campaign Financing Compares to Other Countries

Politicians and political campaigns in the United States far outstrip all other countries in political spending. One of the key reasons for this disparity is the cost of media advertising in the United States. Many other countries, especially those in Europe, limit the amount of advertising a candidate can spend on television and other advertising.

Countries with no campaign spending limits, such as Australia, Germany, Spain, and Turkey, do not necessarily have higher levels of campaign spending. U.S. campaign spending is higher in proportion to the population than that of countries that have no limits on campaign spending. However, in no-limit countries various factors affect reduced campaign spending. These factors include spending limits on media advertising. Some countries, such as Norway, even ban television advertising entirely. Others, like Great Britain and Ireland, make a certain amount of TV advertising time available to all candidates and parties equally. These countries also have substantial public funding programs in place and restrictions on how long a candidate can campaign.

Countries such as Canada, Japan, and Ireland do impose spending limits, as the United States does. However, these limits are typically much lower than what is allowed in America. Other countries, such as Great Britain and Italy, have limits on spending but not on donations to political campaigns. The rationale for this approach is that the limit on spending prevents candidates from seeking larger donations and also helps reduce the influence of large donors on candidates' decisions if they are elected.

For the most part, other countries, especially those in Europe, have made a concerted effort to limit the influence of money in politics. For example, in France there is a higher limit on individual contributions than there is in the United States. However, it is illegal for special-interest groups, such as corporations and unions, to contribute to candidates. In Germany, campaigns are primarily paid for through public funds, although about one-third of campaign contributions come from corporate and individual donors. Germany also places limits on television advertising, allowing each political party only one ninety-second television ad throughout the entire election.

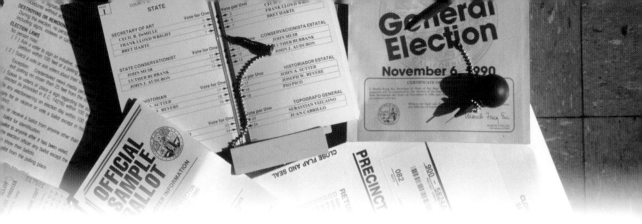

Chapter 3

PACs

The Texas Nationalist Movement wants Texas to succeed from the United States. The National Pest Control Association seeks to promote the pest management industry. In 2010, then–teenagers Zach and Payden Hall wanted to persuade conservative teenagers to become more involved in the political process. Although these groups and individuals have very different goals, they have one thing in common. They all formed political action committees, better known by the acronym PACs.

Almost any group of U.S. citizens and nearly any U.S. organization can form a PAC. As noted by Robert Biersack in the introduction to the book *Risky Business? PAC Decisionmaking in Congressional Elections*, PACs "represent one mechanism through which people who share some common interest can participate as a group in the political process." By pooling the resources of many contributors, PACs can accept small donations and turn them into significant contributions to either directly or indirectly support candidates. PACs can also use the money they raise to promote ideological beliefs, even if their goal is to turn a U.S. state into an independent nation-state.

In 2012, business magnate and philanthropist Sheldon Adelson accounted for 10 percent of all outside donations to political campaigns and PACs. His nearly $100 million in donations was about one-third of 1 percent of Adelson's personal net worth of $37 billion.

A BRIEF HISTORY

The first PAC was formed in 1944, in the midst of World War II, in response to the Smith-Connally Anti-Strike Act of 1943. The law stemmed partly from labor unions striking for higher wages. Because certain segments of industry and manufacturing were crucial to the war effort, a strike could greatly hinder or even shut down a facility or an entire industry. The Smith-Connally Act allowed the federal government to seize control and operate vital industries, if strikes were called.

The Smith-Connally Act also prohibited labor unions, corporations, and interstate banks from contributing to candidates for federal elections. In response to the ban, the Congress of Industrial Organizations (CIO), a powerful labor union, formed a PAC to seek voluntary contributions in support of reelecting President Franklin D. Roosevelt, who was considered a friend of labor. The PAC allowed the CIO to get around the ban on unions contributing to candidates for federal office with money taken from union dues.

The U.S. Congress responded to the CIO PAC by passing the Taft-Hartley Act of 1947. This act banned banks, corporations, and labor organizations from contributing to the campaigns of politicians running for federal office, regardless of how the money was raised. The act also banned contributions for other expenditures, such as efforts involving primary elections, political conventions, and caucuses.

A NEW ERA

The campaign finance portions of the Taft-Hartley Act were largely ignored over the years, due to a lack of enforcement. A comprehensive framework for regulating federal campaign financing went into effect through the Federal Election Campaign Act of 1971. This act, which was amended in 1974 due to the Watergate scandal, was designed to reduce the influence of money in politics. It did this primarily by imposing strict limits on what corporations, unions, or individuals could give to any one candidate.

The new law, however, opened a new era for PACs. Unions and corporations were now allowed to solicit voluntary contributions from members and employees. Union and corporate treasury money could also be used for operating expenses associated with PACs.

By soliciting small contributions from a large number of individuals, PACs were able to provide substantial funds for candidates. What followed was a rapid growth in PACs. The number of PACs increased from 113 in 1972 to 4,009 by 1984. The largest growth was in corporate PACs, which increased from 89 in 1974 to 1,682 in 1984. The surge in dollars contributed to campaigns and other politically orient-

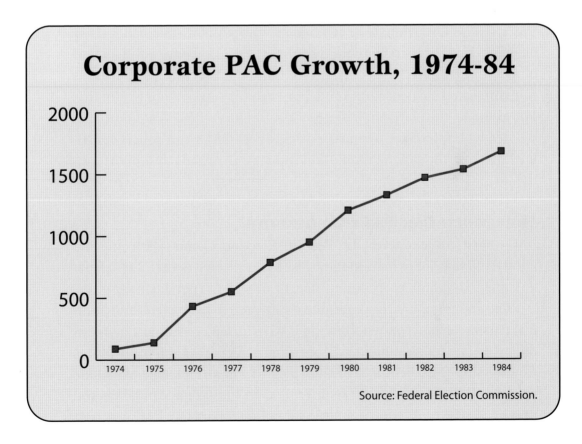

Corporate PAC Growth, 1974-84

Source: Federal Election Commission.

ed efforts went from $19.1 billion in 1972 to more than $267 million in 1984.

The initial growth spurt of PACs eventually slowed down and the number of PACs remains around 4,000 today. Nevertheless, PACs became more and more important as the cost of financing elections skyrocketed. PACs, including what has become known as super PACS, spent more than $2 billion during the 2013–2014 election cycle.

How PACs Are Organized

There are two kinds of PACs: connected and nonconnected PACs. Connected PACs are directly associated with specific organizations, such as companies, labor groups, or political parties. These PACs can only solicit contributions from employees or other members of the organization. In turn, connected PACs can contribute to candidates or political parties.

Nonconnected PACs are sometimes referred to as "ideological" PACs. These PACs donate to candidates who support specific ideals or agendas that are compatible with the PACs' ideals or agendas. Nonconnected PACS are composed of individuals or groups of citizens not connected to a corporation, labor organization, or political party. For example, the National Rifle Association has a PAC to support candidates who favor gun owners' rights. These PACs can solicit contributions from the general public and then use the funds to support candidates.

How Much Can PACs Contribute?

PACs must register with the Federal Election Commission and are allowed to raise only hard money. PACs can receive up to $5,000 from any one individual, party committee, or other PAC per calendar year.

The amount a PAC is allowed to contribute to campaigns and political parties depends on whether the PAC is formed to support one candidate or multiple candidates. According to Federal Communications Commission (FCC) rules, a PAC formed to support a single candidate can contribute up to $2,700 each year to an individual candidate and up to $33,400 each year to a national political party. A PAC can contribute a combined maximum of $10,000 each year to a state, district, or local party committee. Finally, a $5,000 contribution can be made to any other political committee per year.

Multicandidate PACs are allowed to contribute $5,000 each year to an individual candidate, $15,000 each year to a national political party, and $5,000 to any other political committee per year. Multicandidate PACs can also contribute $5,000 each year, combined, to a state, district, or local party committee. The FEC typically adjusts donation limits every two years for the next federal election cycle.

WHY ARE PACs IMPORTANT?

PACs provide access to an extremely valuable campaign commodity—money. When it comes to elections, the candidate who spends the most money usually wins.

In federal elections, as well as in many states, PACs can contribute more money to candidates than individuals can. So if individuals support a certain candidate or agenda, their contributions can have a greater impact when they pool their resources through PACs.

Although limits apply to how much PACs can contribute to a candidate's campaign, there are no limits on how much a PAC can spend independent of a campaign or political party or committee. For example, PACs can spend as much money as they want on advertising in support of or against a candidate or specific agendas.

PACs can use their funds in numerous ways, such as financing get-out-the-vote drives, sponsoring fundraising events, and printing flyers. The vast majority of PAC money, however, is used for television advertising because that has proven so effective in swaying voters' opinions. In the 1988 presidential election, for example, Democratic candidate Michael Dukakis was successfully attacked by a PAC that paid for an ad featuring a murderer.

The convicted murderer, named Willie Horton, had been given a weekend furlough while Dukakis was governor. Horton never returned from the furlough and eventually committed assault, armed robbery, and rape while on the loose before being shot and then captured by police. The "Willie Horton campaign" became infamous for

Leadership PACs

According to the FEC, a leadership PAC is a political committee established, financed, maintained, or controlled by a federal officeholder or a candidate for national office. The Ethics Reform Act of 1989 stated that members of Congress could not convert campaign funds to personal use. Leadership PACs, a type of nonconnected PAC, were created shortly thereafter by the U.S. Congress as a way for members of Congress to use this money while soliciting further donations.

Like other PACs, contributions to leadership PACs are limited to $5,000 a year from an individual donor or another PAC. There are also limits on how much these PACs can donate. Limits vary from about $5,000 to a candidate per election to $10,000 to state parties. The Center for Responsive Politics reported that over 2013–2014, leadership PACs spent approximately $47 million on federal candidates for the 2014 midterm election.

Leadership PACs are prohibited by the FEC from having any official relationship with particular campaigns and from directly campaigning on behalf of the federal officeholder who formed the PAC. Nevertheless, money from these PACs can be used to lay the groundwork for future support by building donor lists, traveling to early primary states, and contributing to local officials and state parties. Potential candidates can also form leadership PACs without formally declaring their candidacy.

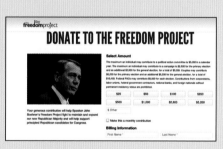

Former Congressman John Boehner's Freedom Project PAC was one of the top-spending PACs in 2015.

In 1994, there were thirty-eight members of Congress with leadership PACs. This number has grown into the hundreds. Leadership PACs became more and more popular as a way to circumvent campaign finance laws. Most of the legislative efforts designed to place restrictions on leadership PACs have failed because of bipartisan support of these PACs among both Democrats and Republicans.

portraying Dukakis as weak on crime—implying that the governor was, in a way, responsible for the crimes Horton committed once he was furloughed. Many analysts believe the ad played a significant role in swaying the election, which was won by the Republican nominee, George H. W. Bush.

Generally, candidates appreciate advertising by PACs. The candidate does not have to pay for an expensive national advertising campaign, like the Willie Horton effort. Perhaps even more important, if the advertisement is subsequently attacked for presenting untruths, the candidate can disavow any association with the ad because the PAC was not directly connected to the candidate's campaign.

STATE-LEVEL PACs

PACs are primarily known for their efforts for and impact on federal elections. PACs, however, also operate on the state level. Thousands of state-based PACs have been established. Various rules and restrictions govern them, according to state election laws. For example, several states have no limit on the amount a PAC can contribute to a candidate's campaign. Unlike PACs on the federal level, state-level PACs do not have to report their contributions and expenditures to the FEC.

State-level PACs primarily focus on local and statewide candidates and issues. These PACs have a wide range of interests. They may support candidates running for all sorts of political offices, from state governors to city mayors to municipal school board candidates. However, many federal-level PACs also have interests in state-level elections and issues. For example, a super PAC named Liberty for All spent $35,000 in a Democratic primary for constable in Travis County, Texas. That expenditure, used primarily for television commercials attacking the incumbent, exceeded the incumbent's entire campaign war chest. "All politics is local at the end of the day," Preston Gates, executive director of the Liberty for All PAC told *USA Today*.

How PACs Benefit Democracy

Whenever money is involved in politics, controversies and disagreements abound. Some people believe that PACs have a positive impact

In 2011, the social media company Facebook formed a PAC. Facebook's PAC, and PACs formed by other Internet companies, focus on supporting candidates favorable to their views on legislative issues, such as concerns about the privacy of users and patent and monopoly laws.

at both the federal and state level because they get more people involved in the political process, thereby strengthening representative government. According to this argument, PACs bring people together for effective political action. Furthermore, PACs are a fair system of raising money for political purposes because PACs are not allowed to coordinate their efforts with candidates.

One of the chief arguments in favor of PACs is that PACs support the First Amendment to the U.S. Constitution, which guarantees freedom of speech. Furthermore, according to proponents of PACs, studies have shown that spending on negative ads actually increases voter knowledge and turnout. Voters who know the least about politics when a campaign begins benefit the most when PACs bring various issues to their attention.

PACs can help underfunded candidates compete against those with a large campaign bankroll. By supporting candidates who have less money for campaigning than their opponents, PACs can help these candidates win an election. In this way, supporters of the current system argue, PACs can create more competition for office and reduce the influence in politics of wealthy individuals and corporations. In addition, some PACs, such as those that support environmental initiatives, perform a valuable public service by bringing various issues, like climate change, to public attention in political campaigns.

PACs "help create buzz and exploit an issue but people need to remember money flowing into campaigns is not new," James Lee, founder of the Lee Strategy Group communications firm told CNBC. "It really comes down to the candidate and their positions."

How PACs Hurt Democracy

Those who oppose PACs offer numerous counterarguments. One of their key contentions is that PACs give special-interest groups too much influence in politics. Essentially, opponents argue, PACs foster a system of buying opportunities to influence politicians' decisions.

Another argument against PACs is that these organizations can influence the partisan or ideological balance in government bodies,

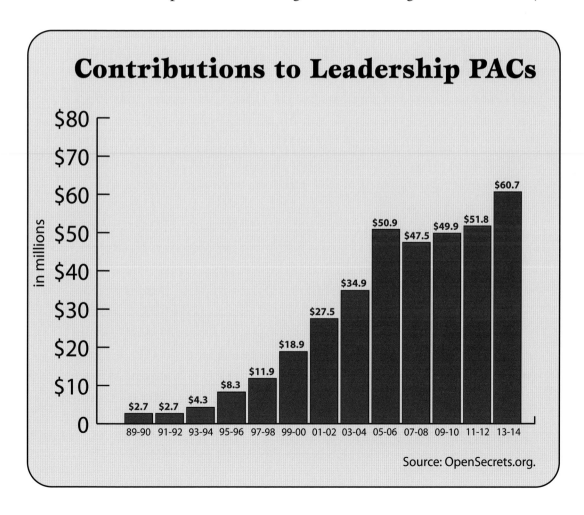

Contributions to Leadership PACs

Source: OpenSecrets.org.

specifically the U.S. House of Representatives and the U.S. Senate. This influence can be for the PACs' own benefit and not necessarily reflect the greater good or the wishes of the general public. For example, some argue that PACs formed by gun advocates to support candidates endorsing gun ownership undermine gun control, which is favored by a majority of Americans.

Another concern is the unlimited spending PACs are able to do as long as they do not coordinate with a candidate's campaign or political committee. Opponents believe that it is naive to think that PACs do not coordinate in any way with a candidate or a candidate's representatives. They argue that decisions by incumbents and challengers, regarding support for or opposition to particular bills or initiatives, are often made outside the public's view and off the record. So it is difficult to gauge the exact role that PACs may have played in such decisions.

PACs may accord undue influence to wealthy individuals and large organizations and companies. More than half of all PACs represent corporations or special-interest groups. Critics also claim that PACs have made it more expensive to run for office, thus giving the wealthy disproportionate influence in our political system. For example, when a PAC supports one candidate, either through direct or indirect funding, the other candidate typically must garner more funding to stay competitive.

Finally, a growing concern is that some PAC money is targeted not for campaigns and political issues but for personal gain. In essence, some PACs may be using contributions for expenditures such as overhead, which may include exorbitant salaries for PAC leaders themselves. Another way PACs may siphon off money, according to critics, is by making large payments to various vendors that are owned by the people who work for the PAC or relatives and friends of PAC leaders. In the 2013–2014 election cycle, a PAC called the Madison Project spent more than $5 million during the campaign cycle. However, only 6 percent, or a little more than $300,000, went to direct contributions or independent expenditures on behalf of a candidate.

Chapter 4

Super PACs

A super PAC is not a superhero, a video game, or an app for a smartphone. Super PACs, however, are "super" in terms of injecting vast sums of money into politics.

At the beginning of the 2015–2016 election cycle, Jeb Bush was competing against a large field of candidates to become the Republican nominee for president. In just several months, the Right to Rise USA Super PAC raised more than $103 million in donations to promote Bush as the Republican nominee. Meanwhile, Bush's official campaign fundraising effort raised only $11.4 million from traditional PACs and other contributors. "It officially ushered in the super PAC era of presidential politics," wrote Politico website contributor Kenneth P. Vogel.

Super PACs had already been making a significant impact in politics. In the 2012 election cycle, philanthropists Sheldon and Miriam Adelson donated nearly $100 million to independent spending groups, most falling into the category of super PACs. In the 2014 mid-term election cycle, billionaire banker Thomas Steyer contributed more than $72 million.

Thanks to his political pedigree (son and brother of two presidents; two-term governor of Florida) Jeb Bush was an early favorite to win the Republican Party's nomination in 2016. In early 2015 he led all candidates in fundraising, and some experts believed that he might raise as much as $2 billion if he won the nomination. But despite his fundraising success, by the end of the year Bush found himself lagging in the polls behind other candidates.

The core controversy surrounding super PACs focuses on two key issues: (1) freedom of speech (and whether monetary donations constitute a form of "political speech") and (2) whether the super wealthy have too much influence in politics. Interestingly, despite the early influx of money supporting his 2016 Republican primary bid, Jeb Bush continued to lag behind in the polls. Several months into his campaign, Bush was ranked third in the polls. Furthermore, in the 2012 presidential election, outside sources of support, primarily in the form of super PACs, spent more than $450 million to bolster Republican candidates. Super PACs spent roughly $350 million in support of Republican Mitt Romney, who lost that election. By contrast, super PACS spent only about $100 million in support of the eventual winner, incumbent Barack Obama.

Such results prove that in deciding the outcome of political campaigns, money is not everything. Still, the impact of super PACs on the electoral process cannot be denied.

A BRIEF HISTORY

Super PACs owe much of their existence to the Supreme Court cases of *Citizens United v. FEC* and *McCutcheon v. FEC*. However, some believe that without the ruling in a lesser-known court case, *SpeechNow.org v. FEC*, there would be no super PACs at all.

SpeechNow.org, a group formed to make independent expenditures in political races, challenged provisions in the Federal Election Campaign Act. Specifically, SpeechNow wanted to exceed the Federal Election Commission limit of $5,000 in individual donations to independent groups. In addition, the organization opposed FEC reporting requirements concerning donors and how much they gave.

In March 2010, the U.S. District Court for the District of Columbia ruled in favor of SpeechNow.org, using the precedent established by the U.S. Supreme Court in *Citizens United v. FEC* earlier in 2010. The District Court in the SpeechNow.org case decided it was unconstitutional for the government to restrict the amount of donations given to an independent organization like SpeechNow.org, deeming them a violation of the First Amendment right of free speech. The *SpeechNow.org* ruling, however, did not affect FEC restrictions on direct contributions to candidates.

The major impact of the Supreme Court's *Citizens United* decision was twofold. The High Court ruled that even an organization that was formed to make independent expenditures still had to register as a PAC. However, the High Court also ruled that independent-expenditure PACs, or super PACs, could accept unlimited contributions from individuals. This made super PACs largely unfettered and unregulated vehicles, compared to regular PACs, in terms of securing large donations and subsequent political spending.

The *Citizens United* and *SpeechNow.org* cases are fundamentally different. SpeechNow.org successfully challenged federal fundraising caps by organizations independent of campaigns, while *Citizens*

United won the right for unlimited spending by corporations, unions, and associations. To put it another way, the Citizens United organization focused on spending money to influence elections while SpeechNow.org focused on raising money for the same end.

THE IMPACT OF SUPER PACs

Super PACs enable fewer donors who write larger checks to essentially bankroll and take over some of the core functions of campaigning. These functions include efforts such as contacting voters and building email lists of voters. Super PACs can also institute a rapid-response effort when a candidate is attacked by the news media or other candidates. Perhaps most important, super PACs can spend huge sums of money on television and other forms of advertising in support of a particular candidate or political agenda.

If they have the backing of super PACs, official campaign committees do not have to spend as much from their coffers to perform key campaign functions. It is estimated that super PACs can provide as much as three-quarters of the costs campaigns traditionally had to cover. For example, in the 2012 Republican presidential primary race, Republican candidate Rick Santorum lagged far behind in fundraising, which hindered his campaign effort. A super PAC—the Red, White and Blue Fund, bankrolled largely by billionaire Foster Friess—helped Santorum stay in the race. The super PAC not only covered the cost of voter outreach efforts in North Dakota, it also aired television ads in favor of Santorum. Santorum won the North Dakota primary with 40 percent of the vote.

Super PACs can also free candidates from focusing on raising large sums of money in small increments. As a result, super PACs have marginalized regular PACs and other fundraising groups that bundle numerous smaller donations. Writing for the *Washington Post*, Matea Gold and Tom Hamburger pointed out: "In the words of one veteran GOP fundraiser, traditional bundlers have been sent down to the 'minor leagues.'" In their place, write Gold and Hamburger, "megadonors are 'the major league players.'"

Colbert for President?

During the 2012 campaign for president, comedian Stephen Colbert established a super PAC called Americans for a Better Tomorrow, Tomorrow. Primarily through his television show, *The Colbert Report*, Colbert raised more than $1 million to support his bogus candidacy for the presidency.

"Comedians, including Mr. Colbert in the last election, have undertaken faux candidacies," noted *New York Times* contributor David Carr. "But his super PAC riff is a real-world exercise, engaging in a kind of modeling by just doing what super PACs do." For example, Colbert's super PAC ran advertising in Iowa prior to that state's primary.

Stephen Colbert won two Emmy Awards in 2013 for his show's political satire.

Like all good satirists, Colbert was doing more than making fun of super PACs and politics. He provided real insight into how super PACs operate and the campaign financing process. "Mr. Colbert has taken the equivalent of a political homework assignment and sprinkled a little silly sauce on top, and people seem happy to dig in," noted Carr.

A 2014 study led by Bruce Hardy of the University of Pennsylvania found that Colbert was extremely successful at educating the public about the intricacies of super PACs. The report, published in the journal *Mass Communication and Society*, stated that a survey of 1,232 adults found that Colbert "not only increased people's perceptions that they knew more about political financing, but significantly increased their actual knowledge, and did so at a greater rate than other news sources." These "other" news sources included Fox News, MSNBC, CNN, and nightly network news broadcasts.

THE PROS AND CONS OF SUPER PACS

The American public has long viewed the influx of money into politics in a negative light. In a 2015 poll conducted by the *New York Times*, 84 percent of the respondents thought money had too much influence in politics. In a 2012 survey conducted for the Brennan Center for Justice at New York University's School of Law, 70 percent of the respondents thought super PAC spending likely would increase corruption in politics. In addition, approximately 75 percent believed that limiting how much corporations, unions, and individuals could donate to super PACs would decrease the chances of political corruption.

Despite the general public's opinion, money in politics remains hotly debated by scholars, the press, candidates' supporters, and the candidates themselves. Both sides see their arguments as valid.

SUPER PACS ARE GOOD FOR DEMOCRACY

One of the primary arguments in favor of super PACs follows the reasoning of those in favor of regular PACs. Super PACs are merely another voice for the people. Being super wealthy does not preclude a person from exercising the right to voice a political opinion.

Proponents of super PACs say that individuals, companies, and unions were already able to get around some campaign finance laws and, thus, were spending unlimited amounts during elections to promote their political agendas. Furthermore, the Supreme Court ruled that independent spending is not likely to have a corrupting influence in politics as long as the groups are not allowed to donate directly to candidates or to perform any function at the request of a candidate. This means they are not allowed to coordinate with candidates or their representatives when it comes to super PAC communications, including issues concerning content, timing, and intended audience.

Supporters of super PACs cite the 2011–2012 election cycle to show that super PACS, at least early on in their formation, have not been a deciding factor in who wins elections. Many candidates who received significant backing from super PACs in 2012 ended up losing their elections. For example, the super PAC called American

During the 2012 presidential election, $1.14 billion was spent in support of the Republican candidate, Mitt Romney, including over $418 million raised by super PACs. The Democratic Party candidate, Barack Obama, benefitted from $964 million in campaign spending, including about $100 million raised and spent by super PACs. The disparity in outside funding helped to offset the Obama campaign's edge in traditional fundraising, as the Democrat collected more than $630 million directly from supporters, compared to $389 million donated to Romney.

Crossroads and its spin-off, a group called Crossroads Grassroots Policy Strategies (Crossroads GPS), spent more than $100 million to support Romney and oppose the Democratic incumbent.

Overall, super PACs and other nonprofits supporting Romney raised much more than those supporting Obama. Super PACs for Romney raised more than $400 million, compared to the $100 million raised by super PACs to help Obama. The fact that Obama won the election, say super PAC proponents, proves that money does not buy votes.

Advocates of super PACs argue that these are not secretive, unregulated organizations. Proponents point to laws that require super PACs to disclose their donors and the amount of money each one gives to the organization. In addition, all expenditures must be reported. Super PACs enable previously underfunded candidates to remain in the race, thus actually reducing big money's influence in politics and allowing more voices to be heard in the political dialogue.

In the 2012 presidential election, thirty-two of the biggest super PAC donors matched the total giving of $313 million by every small-dollar donor to the campaigns of Mitt Romney and Barack Obama. Although donors who gave less than $200 were not disclosed, it is estimated that the number of small donors was at least 3.7 million people.

SUPER PACs ARE BAD FOR DEMOCRACY

A major argument against super PACs is that it is naive to think that the influx of money from wealthy donors does not have an impact on candidates' future decisions if they're elected. In an interview with the *San Antonio Business Journal*, Mimi Marzianai, a lawyer for the Democracy Program at New York University, noted: "It defies logic" to believe that large donations by individuals do not lead a candidate to "feel indebted to that individual in some way."

Those opposed to super PACs also believe that the disclosure requirements associated with super PACs are largely ineffective. Oversight is minimal, they argue, and there are numerous ways to get around most restrictions. For example, due to a technicality in disclosure rules, donors to super PACs can remain anonymous for months.

In addition, super PACs have circumvented all donor disclosure rules by forming affiliated nonprofit 501(c)(4) social welfare organizations, which do not have to release the names of their donors. A social welfare organization operates primarily for the public good in a community or in the nation. These organizations can still engage in lobbying efforts and other political activities on the federal level, as long as that is not the organization's principal activity. American Crossroads is a well-known 501(c)(4) organization that supports conservative candidates, while Organizing for Action is a 501(c)(4) organization that supports liberal candidates.

When full disclosure of donors and the amount they contribute is not mandatory, argue opponents, voters often have no idea about the sources of campaign spending. So, for example, when a super PAC runs a negative campaign commercial on television, voters have no way to judge the fairness of the ad based on who is donating to the super PAC. Therefore, voters' ability to make an informed judgment is compromised. Money donated from unknown sources is typically called "dark money." In addition, shareholders of corporations do not know much about a company's political contributions and spending, which might influence their investment in the company if they do not agree with the company's political stance.

Another problem involves drawing a distinction between coordinated and independent super PACs. Because of modern media saturation in political campaigns, it is no longer clear what it means to say a super PAC is independent of a campaign. Because candidates and their representatives can widely disseminate candidates' views in interviews, in debates, and on the Internet, it is easy for a super PAC to figure out what candidates want and what candidates think will help them most.

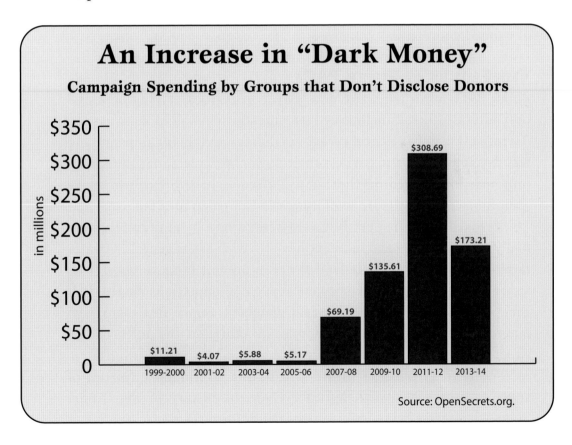

An Increase in "Dark Money"

Campaign Spending by Groups that Don't Disclose Donors

Source: OpenSecrets.org.

In addition, opponents point out that super PACs are often run by candidates' friends and allies. These individuals already have consulted with candidates and have access to candidates beyond the role of the super PACs. For example, the Restore Our Future super PAC, which supported Mitt Romney in the 2012 presidential election, was run by former Romney aides. And a former White House spokesman and other Barack Obama allies created the Priorities USA Action Super PAC in support of Obama.

Yet another argument against super PACs is that they promote the influence of corporations, to the detriment of small businesses. Furthermore, some argue that super PACs undermine the electoral process. For example, attack ads may be distasteful and may contain untruths designed to sway or confuse voters. Finally, super PACs might change the dynamics of the election process itself. Candidates no longer must first appeal to their constituents but rather to the extremely wealthy, thus placing rich donors' concerns over the general public's concerns.

THE FUTURE OF SUPER PACS

Super PACs are a relatively new player in politics, having appeared only after 2010. Although they have already spent significant money during subsequent election cycles, candidates and their campaigns are still developing ways to harness their power. Because super PACs have only recently arrived on the campaign scene, it is difficult to gauge their impact on the future of politics and campaign fundraising.

Some believe that super PACs are here to stay. In addition, they are likely to infuse more and more money into each election cycle. Greater numbers of candidates in federal elections are turning to support from super PACs. These candidates view super PAC support as necessary if they are to compete in elections financially. Super PACs are now embedded in the political economic structure, so the influence of super PACs may just be beginning.

The primary obstacle to the growth and continued influence of super PACs are campaign reforms. Over the history of the United States, there have been various campaign reform efforts.

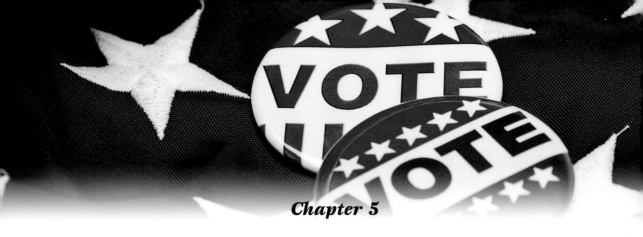

Chapter 5

Campaign Finance Reform

A letter carrier named Douglas Hughes landed a gyrocopter on the White House lawn on April 15, 2015. Hughes was immediately arrested for what turned out to be an unusual protest. Hughes was angry about the outcome of the *Citizens United v. FEC* case of 2010, in which the Supreme Court essentially ruled that money was a form of "political speech." To Hughes, this decision gave the wealthy an unfair advantage in politics and government. Hughes had 535 letters in his possession when he landed on the White House lawn, the exact number needed to give to each member of Congress.

Numerous court decisions and campaign laws have led to unfettered involvement by the wealthy in political campaigns. Thanks to the creation of super PACs and other political organizations, these wealthy individuals can provide nearly unlimited support to candidates without directly contributing to the candidate's campaign.

Several court decisions and laws have changed the political landscape concerning campaign financing. Not everyone supports these new laws and judicial decisions, prompting a new round of debates concerning politics, money, and campaign finance reform.

Reform Is a Failure

Although Hughes, the letter carrier/gyrocopter pilot, is unique in his form of protest, polls have consistently shown that the general public is in favor of campaign finance reform. Nevertheless, various arguments have been presented against reform. These arguments often revolve around the idea that it is unconstitutional to prevent people from using their money as a form of speech. Those who view reform with a wary eye also cite studies concluding that campaign contributions are not a corrupting influence on politicians and the legislative process.

There are, however, other arguments focusing on why campaign reform inherently fails. One such argument is that campaign finance reform produced by legislation and regulations is nearly always futile. Why? Because the legislators creating the laws typically benefit from them, so they have a vested interest in maintaining the status quo. Campaign finance reform was called an "incumbent's protection racket" by *Wall Street Journal* contributor Bradley A. Smith, a law professor who served as commissioner, vice chairman, and chairman of the Federal Election Commission (FEC) between 2000 and 2005.

For example, challengers in elections need to build recognition, which involves spending money for things like TV commercials, travel, and establishing a campaign team. Incumbents already have that recognition and a campaign apparatus in place, thus saving their campaign these initial expenses. Then, as challengers begin to become competitive after spending enough to achieve name and issue recognition on par with incumbents, the challengers get closer to reaching campaign spending limits than the incumbents. As this one-upmanship in campaign fundraising proceeds, political competition is hindered.

Another argument against campaign finance reform is that new legislation to fix loopholes in campaign finance laws often creates new loopholes. These loopholes have increased the influence of special interests. Thus, opponents of reform believe that reform through legislation merely creates more and sometimes different problems. "When a law is in need of continual revision to close a series of ever-changing 'loopholes,' it is probably the law, and not the people, that is in error," wrote Smith in the *Wall Street Journal*.

Activists call for campaign finance reform during a 2015 demonstration in New York City. The "Koch problem" is a reference to wealthy industrialists Charles and David Koch, who have spent hundreds of millions of dollars in recent years to support various conservative politicians and programs. Another billionaire, financier George Soros, has provided similar support to liberal politicians.

Despite its opponents, campaign finance reform is a lot like money in politics; it isn't going to go away. For many who favor reform but agree that true reform is unattainable through the legislative process, the only real campaign finance reform can occur by means of an amendment to the Constitution.

CONSTITUTIONAL REFORM

In mid-2013, U.S. Senator Tom Udall, a Democrat from Utah, introduced a constitutional amendment to reduce the influence of money in politics. The proposed amendment was a direct response to court rulings that essentially led to unlimited donations to super PACs by individuals, as well as companies, labor unions, and other groups.

Udall's proposed amendment would authorize Congress and the states to regulate and limit fundraising and spending on the campaigns of candidates for federal office. In addition, the amendment would not allow the Supreme Court to reverse any future campaign finance legislation passed by Congress. In September 2014 the measure failed to pass in the U.S. Senate.

Enacting an amendment to the constitution is extremely difficult. Any amendment has to be proposed by a two-thirds vote both in the House and in the Senate. The amendment then must be rati-

Senator Lindsey Graham (R-SC) spoke out in 2015 about the need for campaign finance reform. "You're going to have money dumped in this election cycle that's going to turn off the American people," said Graham, a Republican presidential candidate. "There's going to be a need and a movement to try to control the money in politics. We've got to figure out a way to fix this mess, because basically 50 people are running the whole show."

fied by three-quarters of the states. In the years since the ratification of the Constitution in 1788, more than eleven thousand amendments to the Constitution have been proposed. Only twenty-seven have been enacted. So some reform advocates believe that focusing too much on a constitutional amendment distracts from other efforts that are more feasible.

PUBLIC FINANCING

Another route to campaign finance reform is to institute broader public financing of campaigns. Public financing of campaigns has long been available to candidates in various forms. Although most public campaign financing programs are on the state level, the most widely known is the presidential election campaign fund. The fund is publicly supported through a check-off box on federal tax returns. Checking the box allocates $3 from the return to publicly fund presidential candidates. If candidates meet certain qualifications, they are entitled to public funding. If they do not participate, they must limit their fundraising according to federal regulations governing the size and sources of contributions.

Some believe public financing will make officials more accountable to a wider range of American citizens than to special-interest groups and wealthy donors. "The most ideal system would be complete public financing on all elections," comments Craig Holman, a government affairs lobbyist. By "complete," Holman means candidates would not be able accept any other outside contributions.

Arizona and Maine have already instituted what they call "clean elections." In these states, candidates can qualify for state funds only if they forgo all other fundraising and do not accept private funds of any kind. Clean elections also prohibit candidates from using their own personal funds, thus removing an unfair advantage from rich candidates.

In 2015, the U.S. Congress was considering two proposals for public financing of campaign elections. The Government by the People Act focused on putting in place a small-donor matching program for federal elections. The Fair Elections Now Act was designed to enable candidates running for the U.S. Senate to compete by relying on small donations matched by public funds.

Some concerns have also been raised about the growth of super PACs and their effects on publicly funded campaign financing. Although still relatively new, super PACs are steering candidates toward garnering mega donations simply because candidates believe they can raise more money that way. When the dust settles, it might be more difficult to convince candidates to accept public funding if it also places restrictions on other outside funding.

Public funding of presidential campaigns might also disappear. Barack Obama, who opposed super PAC funding, succumbed to the political facts of life by refusing public funding in his 2012 campaign. The reasoning behind this decision was that the limits on public financing placed on campaigns would not allow him to compete on a financial fundraising level with his opponent.

LEGISLATIVE OPTIONS

Because of the *Citizens United* decision and other recent rulings by the Supreme Court, as well as rulings by lower courts, there are limits to what legislation can achieve in campaign finance reform. The Supreme Court essentially decided that political contributions are pro-

A Super PAC for Reform?

Lawrence Lessig, a law professor, formed the Mayday.US Super PAC prior to the 2014 elections. Mayday.US raised nearly $11 million from 68,000 people to support eight congressional candidates who were in favor of campaign finance reform. Most of the candidates supported by Mayday.US lost the election. Lessig subsequently resigned from the PAC so he could run for president during the 2015–2016 election cycle. A foundation of his platform was campaign finance reform.

Believing they learned critical lessons during the 2014 campaign, Mayday.US, under new leadership, set the goal of having a pro-reform Congress after the 2016 elections. The plan included asking members of Congress to become #Leaders4Reform by co-sponsoring reform legislation. Mayday.US supports five campaign reform proposals, two by Republicans, two by Democrats, and one incorporating advice from both sides:

1. The Government by the People Act includes a publicly funded proposal that would match political contributions of up to $150 by a factor of six. Candidates could not use their own money and they could not accept donations of more than $1,000.
2. The American Anti-Corruption Act, developed by a bipartisan team, is aimed at overhauling lobbying and ethics laws and ending secret dark-money contributions.
3. The Political Money Reform Proposal focuses on removing all political spending and contributions, enacting a public elections finance system, and instituting real-time and searchable online reporting of contributions.
4. The Empowering Citizens Act proposes the end of individual candidate super PACs, stronger rules prohibiting coordination between super PACs and candidates, and enhanced judicial review of violations of all campaign financing laws.
5. The Taxation Only with Representation Act proposes that each taxpayer be allowed to earmark the first $200 of a tax payment to support the election of one or more candidates.

tected by the First Amendment right to free speech. Under this reasoning, legislation that limits contributions constitutes an attack on free speech. If the courts continue to support *Citizens United*, significantly addressing campaign finance reform will become an even more difficult proposition.

Nevertheless, legislation can still have an impact on campaign finance reform. For example, instead of seeking to limit contributions, the proposed American Anti-Corruption Act includes provisions to increase transparency and overhaul lobbying and political ethics laws.

In addition to increased small-donor financing, the Empowering Citizens Act, introduced in Congress in 2013, includes a provision to strengthen rules prohibiting coordination between candidates and outside spending groups. The act would also eliminate candidate-specific super PACs, which, according to the law's proponents, typically serve as an arm of the specific candidate receiving super PAC funds. Yet another impact would be to make it illegal for candidates or any of their agents to raise money for super PACs.

Campaign finance reform supporters also look to close dark-money (anonymous donor) loopholes. One suggestion is that any individual or group that spends $10,000 or more on campaign-related expenditures must file a disclosure report with the FEC. Some believe dark money undermines accountability and transparency, which provides voters with important information that can help them make informed decisions.

Corporate donations are also being targeted. The Shareholder Protection Act was proposed to require corporations to disclose all their election-related spending to their shareholders and the general public. Such transparency lets shareholders know if the corporations are making donations to candidates whom individual shareholders do not support.

REGULATE EXISTING LAWS

The Federal Election Commission (FEC) regulates existing laws, including restricting coordination among candidates and outside groups. Nevertheless, a major complaint about campaign financing laws is that they have too many loopholes. In addition, the FEC has failed to be aggressive in enforcing some areas of campaign finance law.

One suggestion for improving FEC oversight is to have FEC commissioner nominations agreed to by a bipartisan group outside of government. At present, the commission is made up of three Republicans and three Democrats. New bipartisan commissioners, argue proponents of this idea, would be more intent on oversight and less concerned with party politics.

Another idea is to have the Internal Revenue Service (IRS) review the status of 501(c)(4)s, which are supposed to be social welfare organizations but might be exploiting their tax-exempt status by engaging primarily in political activity, including an association with super PACs. These groups have been suspected of donating huge amounts of dark money to various political races. Nonprofits like 501(c)(4)s do not have to report the sources of their funding.

A "CONSERVATIVE" APPROACH

According to many conservative politicians, typical approaches to campaign finance reform are misguided. One conservative idea is not to limit funding, but to increase the number of people making small donations.

"There's no question that we live in a nation full of people who are rightfully suspect of the pay-to-play nature of American politics," wrote John Pudner, a conservative political consultant, in an opinion piece for the Moyers & Company website. "That's why incentives must be explored to inspire fellow citizens to open up their minds (and their wallets) to be a part of the solution."

One way to do that, Pudner and some other conservatives assert, is to offer tax credits for contributing money to a campaign. According to Pudner, a $200 tax credit to be allocated to campaign financing might result in $46 billion in small contributions annually if 230 million eligible citizens participated in the plan to its limit.

Another conservative approach is to raise limits at which donors' names must be reported. By doing this, some donors may be more likely to contribute because they would not worry about appearing on some kind of government "list." As an example, proponents point to how potential jury duty lists were once drawn from voter registration lists. As a result, some people would not register to vote because they did not want to be called for jury duty. The laws were changed to gather names from driver license registrations.

THE FUTURE OF CAMPAIGN FINANCE REFORM

If a crystal ball were available to look into the future, the future of campaign finance reform would be cloudy. Although politicians often profess to support public expectations concerning campaign finance reform, little legislation had been

Conservatives like Ted Cruz (R-TX) believe that limits on political donations restrict free speech. Cruz has noted that fundraising restrictions help incumbent politicians, who benefit from lobbyists and special interest money.

passed to institute any genuine reform. The problem, as some see it, is that incumbents from both parties depend on the system already in place.

Some people think the best chance for reform is to make reforms on the state level. For example, Arizona, Vermont, Maine, and Massachusetts all passed campaign finance reform laws. These laws include voluntary public financing of state and local elections. Overall, as of 2015, thirteen states provided some public financing option for campaigns

Many believe that a state-by-state strategy may be the best hope for meaningful campaign finance reform that could ultimately reach the federal level. "It is the states that serve as laboratories of democracy in regard to campaign finance reform," wrote Donald August Gross and Robert K. Goidel in their book titled *The States of Campaign Finance Reform*.

Chapter Notes

p. 6   "or any persons ..." James Fuller, "From George Washington to Shaun McCutcheon: A Brief-ish History of Campaign Finance Reform." *Washington Post* (August 3, 2014). http://www.washingtonpost.com/news/the-fix/wp/2014/04/03/a-history-of-campaign-finance-reform-from-george-washington-to-shaun-mccutcheon/.

p. 6   "money, meat, drink ..." Ibid.

p. 13   "Big money without the right message ..." Bob Shrum, quoted in Stephen J. Dubner, "How Much Does Campaign Spending Influence the Election? A Freakonomics Quorum." Freakonomics (January 17, 2012). http://freakonomics.com/2012/01/17/how-much-does-campaign-spending-influence-the-election-a-freakonomics-quorum/.

p. 25   "represent one mechanism ..." Robert Biersack, Paul S. Herrnson, and Claude Wilcox, eds., *Risky Business: PAC Decisionmaking in Congressional Elections* (Armonk, NY: M.E. Sharpe, 1994), 4.

p. 31   "All politics is local at the end of the day," Preston Gates, quoted in Fredreka Schouten, "Federal Super PACS Spend Big on Local Elections," *USA Today* (February 15, 2014). http://www.usatoday.com/story/news/politics/2014/02/25/super-pacs-spending-local-races/5617121/.

p. 33   "help create buzz and exploit an issue ..." James Lee, quoted in Mark Koba, "Why PACs, Super PACs Dominate the Political Landscape," CNBC website (March 5, 2012); http://www.cnbc.com/id/46341236.

p. 35   "It officially ushered in ..." Kenneth P. Vogel, "Dawn of the Planet of the Super PACs," Politico.com (July 9, 2015). http://www.politico.com/story/2015/07/dawn-of-the-super-pac-era-119936

p. 38   "In the words of one veteran ..." Matea Gold and Tom Hamburger, "In 2016 Campaign, the Lament of the Not Quite Rich Enough," *Washington Post* (March 25, 2015). http://www.washingtonpost.com/politics/in-2016-campaign-the-lament-of-the-not-quite-rich-enough/2015/03/24/f0a38b18-cdb4-11e4-8a46-b1dc9be5a8ff_story.html.

p. 38   "mega-donors are 'the major league players.'" Ibid.

p. 39   "Comedians, including Mr. Colbert ..." David Carr, "Comic's PAC Is More Than a Gag," *New York Times* (August 21, 2011): B1.

p. 39   "Mr. Colbert has taken the ..." Ibid.

p. 39   "not only increased people's perceptions ..." Bruce W. Hardy, Jeffrey A. Gottfried, Kenneth M. Winneg, and Kathleen Hall Jamieson, "Stephen Colbert's Civics Lesson: How Colbert Super PAC Taught Viewers about Campaign Finance," *Mass Communication and Society* 17, no. 3 (2014): 39–353.

p. 42   "It defies logic ..." Mimi Marzianai, quoted in Kent Hoover, "Super PACs Are Changing the Electoral Landscape," San Antonio Business Journal (February 10, 2012). http://www.bizjournals.com/sanantonio/print-edition/2012/02/10/super-pacs-are-changing-the-electoral.html.

p. 46   "incumbent's protection racket," Bradley A. Smith, "Why Campaign Finance Reform Never Works," *Wall Street Journal* (March 19, 1997): A19.

p. 46   "When a law is in need of continual revision ..." Ibid.

p. 48   "You're going to have money dumped ..." Lindsey Graham, quoted in Andy Sullivan, "Here's One White House Hopeful Who Wants to Get Big Money out of Politics," Reuters (April 18, 2015). http://www.reuters.com/article/2015/04/18/us-usa-election-money-idUSKBN0N90SY20150418?feedType = RSS&feedName = politicsNews#kqZR8BqxZkR6oZD2.97

p. 49   "The most ideal system ..." Craig Holman, quoted in Megan Donley, "Affecting Change through Campaign Finance Reform," *South Source* (April 2011). http://source.southuniversity.edu/affecting-change-through-campaign-finance-reform-38736.aspx.

p. 52   "There's no question that we live ..." John Pudner, "Conservative Campaign Finance Reform Increases Participation," Moyers & Company (February 27, 2015). http://billmoyers.com/2015/02/27/conservative-campaign-finance-reform-increases-participation/

p. 53   "It is the states that serve as laboratories ..." wrote Donald A. Gross and Robert K. Goidel, *The States of Campaign Finance Reform* (Columbus: Ohio State University Press, 2003), 102.

Chronology

1867 The first federal campaign law—the Naval Appropriations Act, which forbids politicians and their political parties from requesting political donations from naval yard workers—is passed.

1883 The Civil Service Reform Act applies the Naval Appropriations Act to all government workers.

1896 The presidential election represents a watershed for campaign finance in presidential elections, with William McKinley spending $7 million on campaigning.

1905 President Theodore Roosevelt calls for a ban on corporate contributions to political campaigns.

1913 Passage of the Seventeenth Amendment requires direct election of senators, thus requiring campaign financing.

1944 The first political action committee, or PAC, is formed by the Congress of Industrial Organizations, a labor union, to garner funds through voluntary contributions, rather than union treasury funds.

1947 The Taft-Hartley Act places a ban on contributions to federal candidates from corporations, interstate banks, and unions.

1971 The Federal Election Campaign Act is passed, setting limits on spending by candidates on campaigns, requiring full and timely disclosures of campaign contributions, and limiting some contributions; it also provides for the public financing of presidential campaigns.

1974 Congress creates the Federal Election Commission to enforce the Federal Election Campaign Act provisions.

1976 The U.S. Supreme Court, in *Buckley v. Valeo*, rules that mandatory spending limits violate the guarantee of free speech.

1978 General election spending increases to $153.5 million.

1988 General election spending has increased over the decade to $408.3 million.

2002 The Bipartisan Campaign Reform Act, cosponsored by Democratic Senator Russell Feingold and Republican Senator John McCain, prohibits unregulated, or soft money, contributions to national political parties.

2010 A Supreme Court ruling in the case of *Citizens United v. FEC* prohibits the government from restricting independent political expenditures by a nonprofit corporation. In addition, a District Court case, called *Speechnow.org v. FEC*, strikes down limits on contributions to independent-expenditure political organizations and paves the way for the creation of super PACs.

2012 An estimated $6.2 billion is spent on races for president and Congress.

2014 Roughly $4 billion is spent on campaigns for the 2014 midterm elections; 94 percent of the largest spenders in races for the House of Representatives won and 82 percent of the biggest spenders in Senate campaigns won.

Glossary

501(c)(4)s—tax-exempt nonprofit organizations that can provide political donations as long as social welfare is the organization's main goal and not political participation.

aggregate limit—the maximum dollar amount allowed.

bipartisan—agreement or cooperation between two political parties that have opposing policies and ideological beliefs.

constituency—voters in a particular area who vote in elections for specific offices.

FEC—the Federal Election Commission, which oversees and enforces federal election laws and acts.

incumbent—someone who holds a political office and is campaigning for reelection.

independent expenditures—money spent in support of a political candidate or a political issue by groups without coordinating activities with a particular candidate.

Industrial Revolution—a period of transition over the eighteenth and nineteenth centuries in which America's predominantly agrarian and rural society became industrial and urban.

leadership PAC—a special PAC formed by members of Congress that allows them to use leftover campaign funds in specific ways.

loophole—an ambiguity, often unintentional, in a law or a legal agreement, which allows an individual or corporation to get around the intent of the law, agreement, or regulation.

midterm election—in federal politics, the election cycle that does not include election of the U.S. president.

PAC—a political action committee formed in support of candidates and specific issues.

partisan—a strong supporter of a party, cause, or person.

super PAC—a political action committee that can raise unlimited funds from contributors and is not limited in how much money it can spend in support of a candidate as long as there is no coordination between the candidate's official campaign and the super PAC.

Further Reading

Bardes, Barbara, Mack Shelly, and Steffen Schmidt. *American Government and Politics Today: Essentials 2015-16 Edition*. Boston: Cengage Learning, 2015.

Gerdes, Louise I. *Super PACs*. Detroit: Greenhaven Press, 2014.

Handlin, Amy. *Dirty Deals? An Encyclopedia of Lobbying, Political Influence, and Corruption*. Santa Barbara, Calif.: ABC-CLIO, 2014.

La Raja, Raymond J. *Small Change: Money, Political Parties, and Campaign Finance Reform*. Ann Arbor: University of Michigan Press, 2008.

Mutch, Robert E. *Buying the Vote: A History of Campaign Finance Reform*. New York: Oxford University Press, 2014.

Smith, Melissa M., Glenda C. Williams, Larry Powell, and Gary A. Copeland. *Campaign Finance Reform: The Political Shell Game*. Lanham, Md.: Lexington Books, 2010.

Internet Resources

http://www.cfinst.org

The Campaign Finance Institute's website includes sections covering campaign finance history, federal and state campaign financing, small donors, and the law.

http://www.fec.gov

The Federal Election Commission (FEC) is an independent regulatory agency created to enforce the provisions of campaign laws and oversee the funding of presidential elections.

http://www.brennancenter.org/issues/money-politics

Operated by the Brennan Center for Justice, the "Money in Politics" website provides news about campaign financing.

https://www.opensecrets.org

This website is operated by the nonpartisan Center for Responsive Politics, which focuses on tracking money in U.S. politics and its effect on elections and public policy.

http://sunlightfoundation.com

The website of the Sunlight Foundation, a nonpartisan, nonprofit organization, focuses on transparency in the flow of political money.

Index

Numbers in **bold italic** refer to captions.

About the Author

David Petechuk is a freelance researcher and writer who primarily writes educational books, articles, and encyclopedia entries. He writes for both adults and middle school students. His books include *The Undead: Vampires, Zombies, and Other Strange Monsters* (Eldorado Ink, 2015); *The Respiratory System* (Greenwood Press, 2004), *LSD* (Lucent Books, 2005), and *Non-Continental States: Alaska, Hawaii* (Mason Crest, 2015).

PHOTO CREDITS: Freedom Project: 30; Internal Revenue Service: 21; Library of Congress: 7, 9; OTTN Publishing: 22, 27, 33, 43; Andrew Cline / Shutterstock.com: 36, 53; Rob Crandall / Shutterstock.com: 17 (right); Helga Esteb / Shutterstock.com: 39; Gurganus Images / Shutterstock.com: 17 (left); Juli Hansen / Shutterstock.com: 18; Glynnis Jones / Shutterstock.com: 4; A. Katz / Shutterstock.com: 1, 15, 47; Charlotte Purdy / Shutterstock.com: 41 (left); Joseph Sohm / Shutterstock.com: 11, 41 (right); Jordan Tan / Shutterstock.com: 6; Albert H. Teich / Shutterstock.com: 48; Ken Wolter / Shutterstock.com: 32. Front cover: Rena Schild / Shutterstock.com (left); Mark Poprocki / Shutterstock.com (right top); A. Katz / Shutterstock.com (right bottom). Back cover: used under license from Shutterstock, Inc.